TANNER, G.

Toys

Please return or renew this item by the last date shown.
You may renew items (unless they have been requested
by another customer) by telephoning, writing to or calling
in at any library. ♻ 100% recycled paper   *BKS 1 (5/95)*

Toys

Gill Tanner and Tim Wood

Photographs by Maggie Murray

Illustrations by Pat Tourret

A & C Black · London

Here are some of the people you will meet in this book.

The Hart family in 1990

The Cook family in 1960

Bill Hart

Linda Hart

Kerry

Lee

David Cook

June Cook

Susan

Linda

Andrew

Lee Hart is the same age as you.
His sister Kerry is eight years old.
What is Lee's mum called?

This is Lee's mum Linda when she
was just nine years old in 1960.
She is with her mum and dad,
her brother and her baby sister.

2

The Smith family in 1930

Richard Smith

Lucy Smith

May

Jack and June

The Barker family in 1900

Charles Barker

Alice Barker

Fred

Harry

Lucy

Amy and Adam

This is Lee's granny June
when she was just a baby in 1930.
Her brother Jack is looking after her.

This is Lee's great grandma Lucy
when she was six years old in 1900.
Can you see what her sister
and her brothers are called?

Can you spot the differences between these two photographs?

One shows a modern child playing with a toy
and one shows a child playing with a toy
one hundred years ago.

This book is about toys.
It will help you find out
how toys have changed
in the last one hundred years.

There are ten mystery objects in this book
and you can find out what they are.
They will tell you about people in the past.

In 1900, Lucy Barker loved playing with these.
The smaller object is about the same size as an egg.
It needs the other object to make it work.
What do you think these objects are?

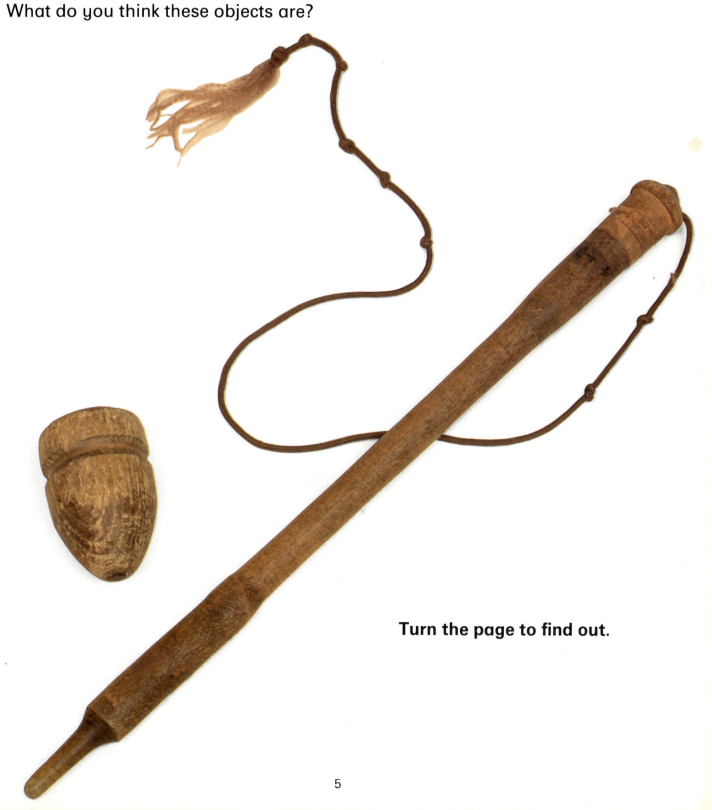

Turn the page to find out.

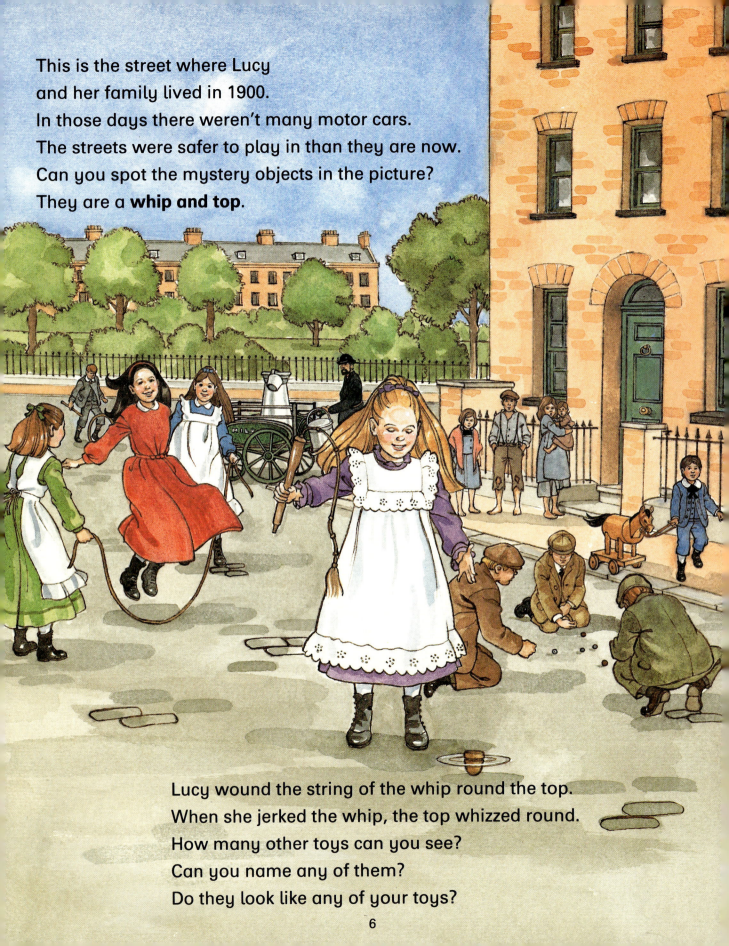

This is the street where Lucy
and her family lived in 1900.
In those days there weren't many motor cars.
The streets were safer to play in than they are now.
Can you spot the mystery objects in the picture?
They are a **whip and top**.

Lucy wound the string of the whip round the top.
When she jerked the whip, the top whizzed round.
How many other toys can you see?
Can you name any of them?
Do they look like any of your toys?

6

These were Fred's toys in 1900.

The toys are about the same size as they are on this page.

You can probably guess what they are,

but do you know what they are made of?

Turn the page to find out.

Fred is playing with his **toy soldiers**.
They were made of a metal called lead.
He had some other lead toys as well.
Can you see them in the picture?
Fred's favourite lead toy was the broken sailor.
Lead is soft and bendy,
so the toys were easily broken.

In those days lots of toys were made of lead.
Most parents did not know that lead was
poisonous and could make children ill.
You might have some toys like these.
Do you know what they are made of?

All the Barker family liked to play with this toy.

It is about as big as this book.

Can you guess what it is?

Turn the page to find out.

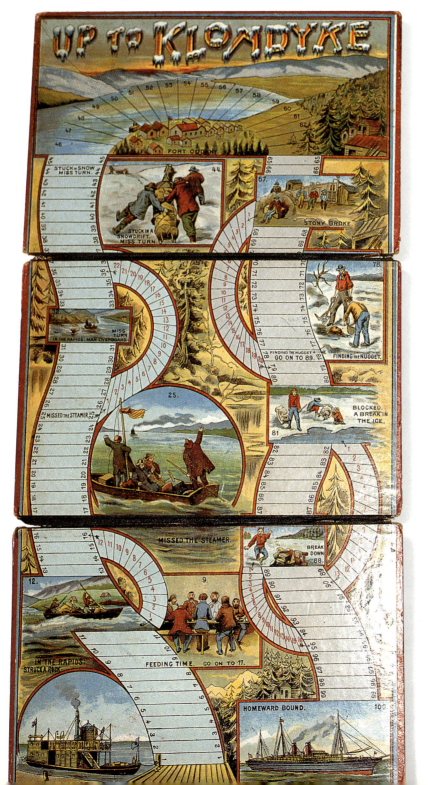

It's raining outside, so Lucy and her family
are all staying indoors.
Can you spot the mystery object?
It's a **board game**.

In those days there were no televisions,
so people had to amuse themselves.
They sang songs around a piano,
read books or played games.
In 1900, board games were very popular.
Do you know any good ones?

This toy belonged to Jack Smith in 1930.
It has lots of different bits which fit together.
The parts are a bit larger than they are on this page.

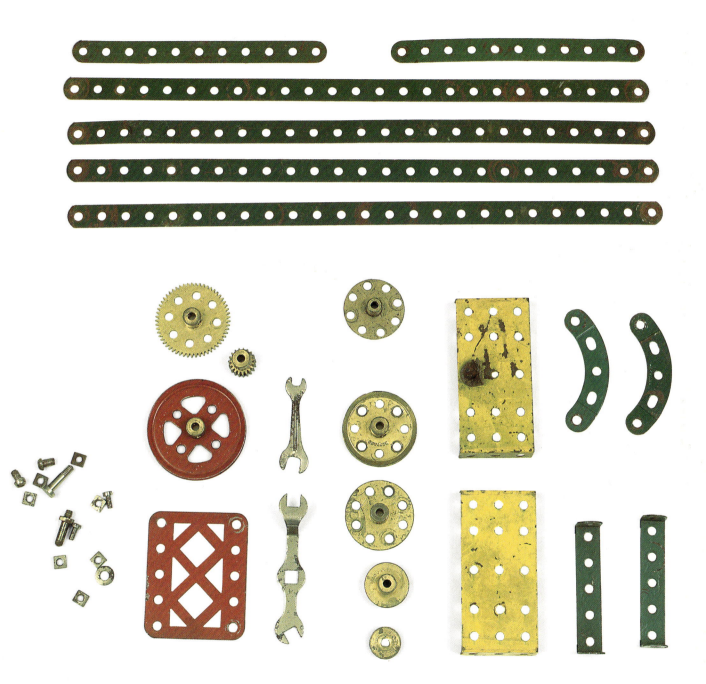

Have you ever seen anything like them?
What do you think they are for?

Turn the page to find out.

The Smiths have just finished supper.
Jack is playing with his toy.
It is a **Meccano set**.

The set had lots of different metal parts.
They were used to build models.
Jack and his dad fixed the parts together
using tiny nuts and bolts.
They are building a crane.
Can you see what Jack is holding?

These objects are the same size
as they are shown on this page.
They are all made of metal.
They are not toys.
But lots of toys in 1930 would not work without them.

Turn the page to find out what they are.

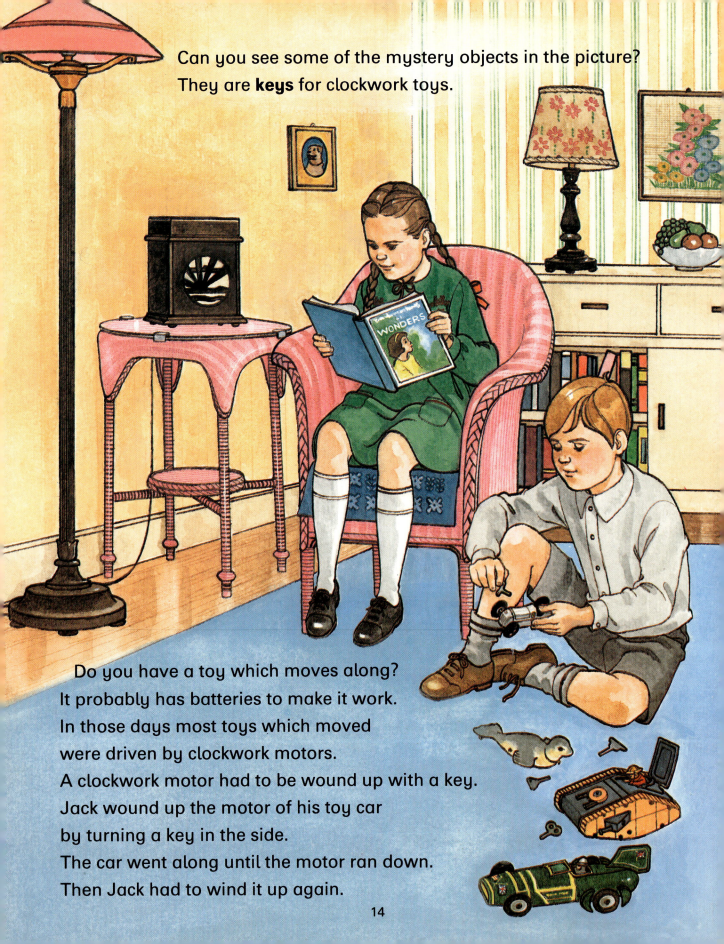

Can you see some of the mystery objects in the picture?
They are **keys** for clockwork toys.

Do you have a toy which moves along?
It probably has batteries to make it work.
In those days most toys which moved
were driven by clockwork motors.
A clockwork motor had to be wound up with a key.
Jack wound up the motor of his toy car
by turning a key in the side.
The car went along until the motor ran down.
Then Jack had to wind it up again.

14

You can probably guess what this mystery object is.
But what do you think it is made from?

Turn the page to find out.

Can you see the mystery object?
When May was younger
it was her favourite **doll**.
Now she has given it to June.

The doll was made of sawdust and glue.
In those days there was no plastic.
Dolls were made of wood, sawdust, cloth, china or wax.
What other toys can you see in the picture?

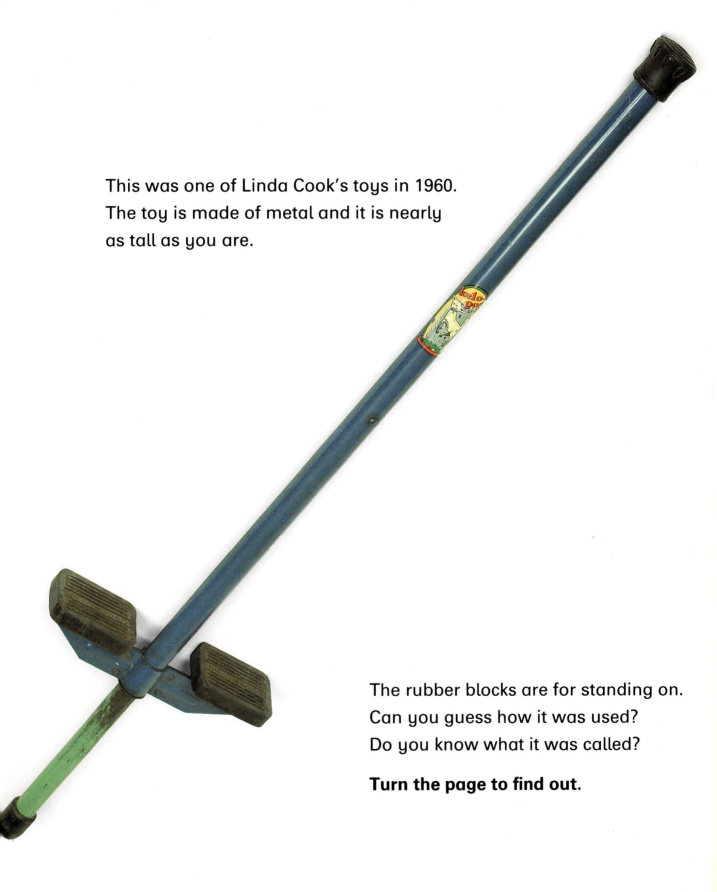

This was one of Linda Cook's toys in 1960.
The toy is made of metal and it is nearly
as tall as you are.

The rubber blocks are for standing on.
Can you guess how it was used?
Do you know what it was called?

Turn the page to find out.

Can you spot the mystery object?
It's a **pogo stick**.
Linda held on to the handle
and stood on the crossbar.
When she jumped up and down
a spring inside the handle
made the pogo stick bounce along.

Linda liked to see how long she
could bounce for before falling off.

How many other toys can you see in the park?
Do you know what they are?

This was part of Andrew Cook's favourite toy.
It made something move along.
Look very closely.
You may spot some writing
which will give you a big clue.
Can you guess what this mystery object is?

Turn the page to find out.

19

Andrew is playing with his electric train set.
Can you see the mystery object in the picture?
It is a **controller**.

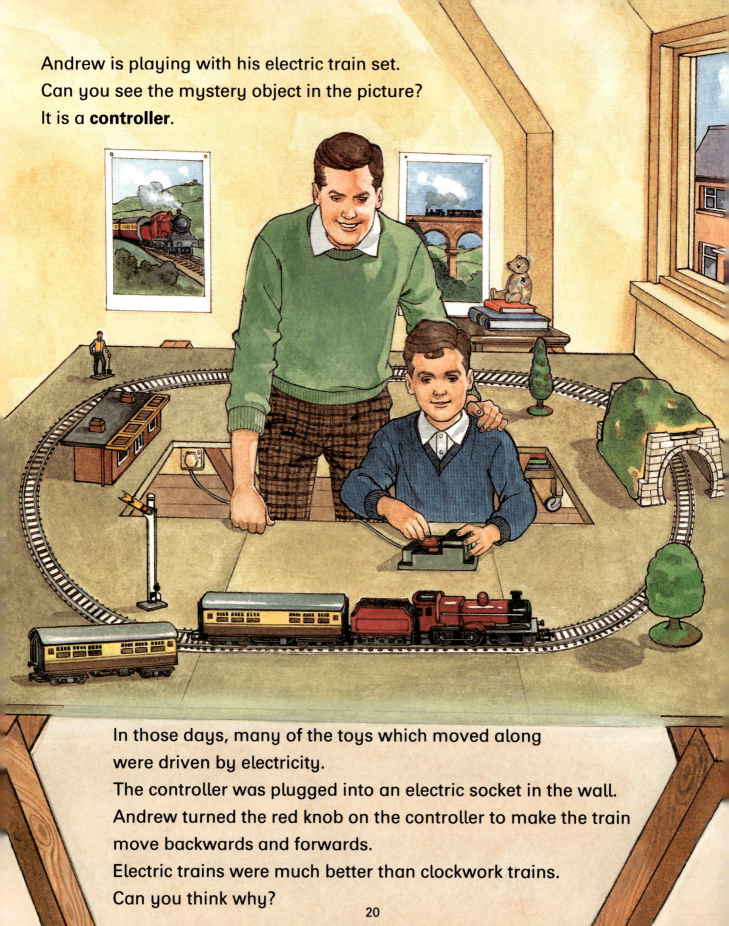

In those days, many of the toys which moved along
were driven by electricity.

The controller was plugged into an electric socket in the wall.

Andrew turned the red knob on the controller to make the train
move backwards and forwards.

Electric trains were much better than clockwork trains.

Can you think why?

20

Now that you know a bit more about toys
and how they have changed over the last hundred years,
see if you can guess what this mystery object is.
It is a toy for very young children.
Adam Barker played with it when he was a baby.
Can you guess what it is made of?

You will find the answer on page 24.

Time-Line

These pages show you the objects in this book and the objects children play with nowadays.

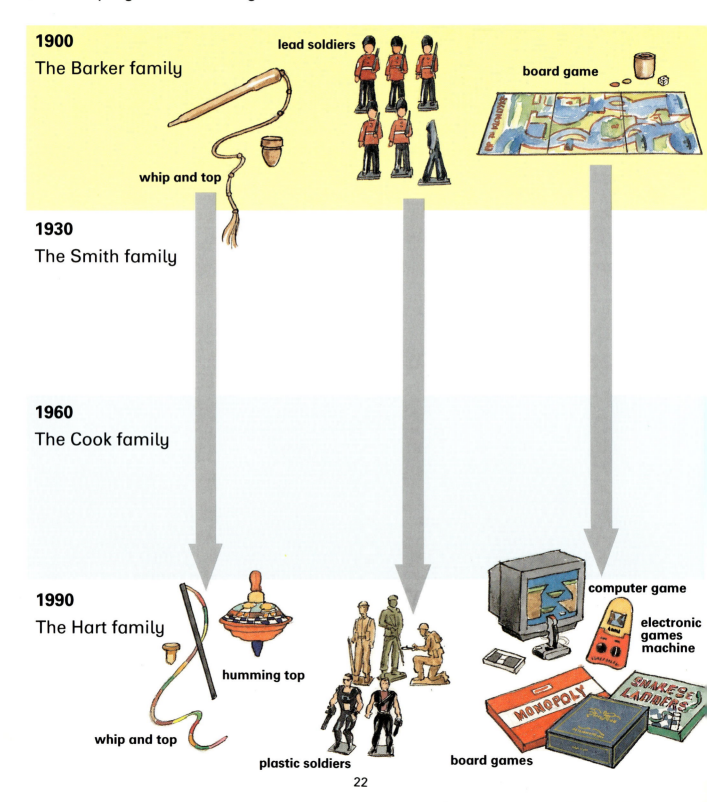

1900
The Barker family

lead soldiers

board game

whip and top

1930
The Smith family

1960
The Cook family

1990
The Hart family

humming top

whip and top

plastic soldiers

computer game

electronic games machine

MONOPOLY

SNAKES & LADDERS

board games

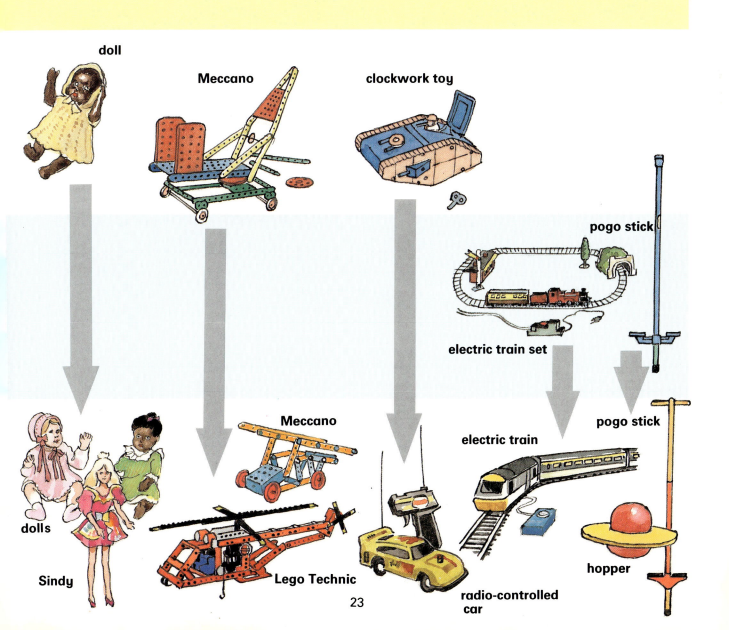

doll

Meccano

clockwork toy

pogo stick

electric train set

dolls

Meccano

Sindy

Lego Technic

electric train

pogo stick

radio-controlled
car

hopper

23

Index

The **mystery object** on page 21 is a **set of bone teething toys**. Adam Barker chewed on them when he was teething. The bone toys helped to cool his hot gums.

For parents and teachers

More about the objects and pictures in this book

Pages 5/6   The Barker family lived in a large industrial town. Tops are very old toys. Children played with them in Ancient Greece. Toys were very expensive in Victorian times and most children had only a few. There were few mass-produced toys.

Pages 7/8   Lead is soft and bendy and good for making models, but because it is poisonous, it's no longer used for toys. Early lead toys were called tin toys, as in tin soldiers. The soldiers were models of British soldiers. In the 1960s, plastic replaced lead as the main model-making material.

Pages 9/10   Board games were first played in Ancient Egypt. Games such as Snakes and Ladders became popular in Victorian times as mass-production made them cheaper. Few parents played with their children – poor parents had little free time, and rich parents left their children with a nanny.

Pages 11/12   The Smiths lived in a semi-detached house in a small town. Meccano, invented in 1901, was the forerunner of modern construction toys such as 'technical' Lego. Although the parts were painted, they often rusted. Meccano kits were expensive.

Pages 13/14   Clockwork motors were powered by an unwinding spring. They were noisy, ran down quickly and were easily damaged by overwinding.

Pages 15/16   Dolls are among the oldest toys. The first recorded doll's house was made in 1558. The first doll's pram was made in 1733 for the Duke of Devonshire and was designed to be pulled by a dog.

Pages 17/18   The Cooks lived in one of the new towns built in the 1960s. Pogo sticks, along with hula hoops, were the 'craze' toys of the 1960s.

Pages 19/20   Train sets were popular after the steam revolution of the 1840s. Electric train sets were first made in 1897. Few homes had electricity before 1926 when the National Grid was set up.

Things to do

History Mysteries will provide an excellent starting point for all kinds of history work. There are lots of general ideas which can be drawn out of the pictures, particularly in relation to the way toys, clothes, family size and lifestyles have changed in the last 100 years. Below are some starting points and ideas for follow up activities.

1 Work on families and family trees can be developed from the families on pages 2/3, bearing in mind that many children do not come from two-parent, nuclear families. Why do the families in the book have different surnames even though they are related? How have their clothes and hair styles changed over time?

2 Find out more about toys and playing in the past from a variety of sources, including interviews with older people in the community, books and toy museums. Toys weren't the same for everyone. Why not?

3 There is one object which is in one picture of the 1900s, one picture of the 1930s, and one picture of the 1960s. Can you find it?

4 Try making and/or testing some toys similar to those made in Victorian times. Visit a toy museum.

5 Look at the differences between the photographs and the illustrations in this book. What different kinds of things can they tell you?

6 Make your own collection of toys or pictures of toys. You can build up an archive or school museum over several years by encouraging children to bring in old objects, collecting unwanted items from parents, collecting from junk shops and jumble sales. You may also be able to borrow handling collections from your local museum or library service.

7 Encouraging the children to look at the objects is a useful start, but they will get more out of this if you organise some practical activities which help to develop their powers of observation. These might include drawing the objects, describing an object to another child who must then pick out the object from the collection, or writing descriptions of the objects for labels or for catalogue cards.

8 Encourage the children to answer questions. What do the objects look and feel like? What are they made of? What makes them work? How old are they? How could you find out more about them?

9 What do the objects tell us about the people who used them? Children might do some writing, drawing or role play, imagining themselves as the owners of different objects.

10 Children might find a mystery object in their own home or school for the others to draw, write about and identify. Children can compare the objects in the book with objects in their own home or school.

11 If you have an exhibition, try pairing old objects with their nearest modern counterparts. Talk about each pair. Some useful questions might be: How can you tell which is older? Which objects have changed most over time? Why? What do you think of the older objects? What would people have thought of them when they were new? Can you test how well the objects work? Is the modern version better than the older version?

12 Make a time-line using your objects. You might find the time-line at the back of this book useful. You could include pictures in your time-line and other markers to help the children gain a sense of chronology. Use your time-line to bring out the elements of *change* (eg. how toys used to be handmade and expensive, how children had far fewer toys, passed them on in the family and did not throw them away, the gradual development of motors from clockwork to modern rechargeable batteries, plastic, hi-tech toys, disposable toys) and of *continuity* (eg. basic similarities in play since 1900 as a method of learning, accumulating knowledge, and developing motor, co-ordination and social skills).

First published 1993
A & C Black (Publishers) Limited
35 Bedford Row, London WC1R 4JH

ISBN 0-7136-3686-6

© 1993 A & C Black (Publishers) Limited
Reprinted 1994

A CIP catalogue record for this book is available
from the British Library.

Acknowledgements

The authors and publishers would like to thank Mrs Tanner's Tangible History;
Suella Postles and the staff of Brewhouse Yard Museum, Nottingham;
Terry Maltman, R.B.S. Long Eaton, Nottinghamshire; Rita Lee; Meccano,
NES Arnold Limited, West Bridgford, Nottingham; LEGO UK Limited; Hasbro UK Ltd.

Photographs by Maggie Murray except for: p 4 (top) Kirklees Cultural Services;
p 4 (bottom) Judy Harrison, Format Photographers.

Filmset by Rowland Phototypesetting Limited, Bury St Edmunds, Suffolk
Printed and bound in Italy by L.E.G.O.